FOREWORD

Thank you for trying out this book. Poetry seems to be a dying artform these days, and I really appreciate your love for writing, as I hope you can appreciate mine channeled through this work, as well as my others.

As has become my ritual, I have included a short story I wrote at the end of the book. I hope you enjoy.

To those that know me well, friends, loved ones, and family, thank you for inspiring me, helping me through the dark times, and for being part of my life. You all make it worth sticking around, you know who you are. Thank you.

CONTENTS

Foreword
Happy 1
Friends 3
Awaken 5
Cats! 7
Gibberish 9
Things and Stuff 11
To Feel a Fool 13
Dark Depths 15
A Lifetime 17
The Devils Ballroom 19
Cattle Battle 21
Mom 23
Amory 25
Despairing 27
Bopanda 29
Silver Gold Moon 30
Obnoxious Thunder 32
I'm Through 33
Sinking 35
Drowning 37

To My Knees	39
Creation of Sadness	41
Fade Away	43
Heavy Rain	45
Night Cats	47
With Regret	49
Save Me (From Myself)	50
Washed Away	52
Hollow	54
Life Before	57
Here We Go	59
Shower	61
Sacred Silence	63
Staring at the Queen	65
Descent	67
Beatings	69
Another Year	71
Torment of Dreams	73
Solitude	75
Near Oceans	77

HAPPY

I never thought that
I would be happy
Content with my lot
But here I am, smiling

Through struggles, personal
Financial, and internal
For some reason I am smiling
Happy to my core with where I am

I never appreciated who
I am or what I can do
The skills I have that create
Create happiness too

I never thought I would like
Who I am, have validation
I've never been my biggest fan
Always a fair-weather friend

My love for myself is like
A fog, that disappears when
The wind redirects
But I have a new appreciation

I can write, quite well I think
I play instruments reasonably
I am good at my job, I believe
I am worth something to this world

I never thought I had worth

But that has started to change
I never thought I had talent
But here I sit

Proud of myself

FRIENDS

Going through life
You get to know people
Some you like, some are feeble
Some stick around, for longer
Or shorter
Some you may say, become family

Friendship is not one sided
You accept them for who they are
And in turn, they accept you
If this two-way street is blocked
Or one side meanders
Issues arise, and friendship is endangered

Those who are lucky
We lucky few
Have friends that last a lifetime
Some even, from school
Acknowledge what you have
And love who you keep

Someday they may disappear
This is out of our control, at times
Death ever waiting
To claim a mortal soul
But they live on in us
Forever in our hearts

Those that last are precious
Do what you can for them

And let them help you too
For what else is life for
Connections, love, and happiness
Are what we are here to do

AWAKEN

Wake from your slumber
Sleeping demon within
I have been wronged
And need your strength

Awaken, my pet rage
For someone has upset me
Draw your golden swords
And defend my sovereign state

Boil up inside me now
It's alright to feel this way
Dip your tips in poison
Lob them at the enemies, left and right

Stand up, my inner hatred
For someone has me irate
Bellow and groan as you erect
Siege weapons at my gate

Feel your anger, it gives clarity
But only when it passes
Treat it like a charity
Give it to those deserving

But keep the snake coiled inside
Keep the forked togue guided
Keep the venom from your speech
It may well be misguided

For when the red haze passes

It's here you still reside
It's you that must see result
Live with consequences reminded

While you call upon your anger
Remember who's in control
Keep it contained unless
Absolutely necessary, you'll know it in your soul

You still need to live your life
And not put someone in a cemetery
Anger is a tool to use
Not your guiding compass

Use it sparingly and deservedly
Know how to be angry, and differentiate
Between friend or foe, flight or fight
And keep it off your wife, alright?

CATS!

A feline is a fantastic creature
Truly aloof, probably thanks to
The ancient Egyptians treating them
As gods among men
Cats have never forgotten

You see, to have a cat is to have a ruler
You may not know it, it could be subtle
They love you when they want
And you don't dare touch when they don't
They will wake you from slumber as they see fit
But don't disturb Miss Paddy Paws
Or you'll end up cut

Cats you see are truly above any other creature
Others are below them
But pets in the grand picture
Dogs? Pah! What silly creatures
It's true I've seen a cat slap and hurt
The biggest most violent dog
Forever did Tiger have respect
For the cat for doing the job

They lie in our rooms
Sleep on our beds
Make us feed them at any time
That suits them in their heads
I have a cat, she's quite a little princess
She scratches me and draws blood at three

In the morning for some food
I best move quick and not hide
Or my scalp will get it next

If she doesn't feel like food, perhaps a little love
Then she will curl up back to sleep
While I sit there a scared lump
Checking over all tattoos looking
For her damage
She cares not, she's had her lot
Purring on the bed asleep

Our feline rulers will no doubt
One day grow tired of us
They will overthrow our race
Take the world for themselves
In their haste they will forget
Just who used to feed them
That will be their downfall, see
Their pure feline arrogance

GIBBERISH

Sometimes I speak and speak
Never to be heard
Sometimes I feel as though
My voice is on mute
Sometimes I speak and speak
Words into the ether

Sometimes I talk and talk
Truths told or questioned
Words to fall on deaf ears
As a pin onto a floor
Sometimes I wonder at the worth
Of speaking anything at all

Most times I have something to say
Its ignored and perhaps guffawed
Later to return, another voice source
Then the truth or idea is grand
When from me it was all but slammed

Sometimes this makes me irate
Other times deflated
To have one's ideas and words
Simply conflagrate
But when someone else may utter
The very same words repeated
Then the idea is bright and wise

Why didn't I think of that?
Oh, wait, I did indeed

That was my intention
Now it has been taken
Had proper implementation

Sometimes I have words to say
But keep them to myself
Because to have one's ideas proliferate
It seems the must come from another
So rather let them think for themselves
That take credit for my thinking

I have many things to say
But I will keep them hidden.

THINGS AND STUFF

Life is not about worldly possessions
Though they may entice
Or maybe even be enjoyed
Life is more about strife

Work hard to get the stuff you want
But first get what you need
We all need love and friends and food
But not the latest iSeed

Everyone wants to have it all
But few can really afford to
So treasure what you do have
It's more important than you know

I don't want to die one day
Regretting I didn't get the latest phone
The latest shiny electronic stone
To read funnies on the throne

I want to die one day
Knowing I had a life fulfilled
Knowing in my heart I left a mark
On the world

Having things is cool and stuff
But so is having joy
And of course, a proper meal
Instead of having some glass and steel

So remember when you see shiny things

Life is more than that
Life is friends and family and love
Connections in the real

TO FEEL A FOOL

Many times in my life
I have fallen in love
Many times in my life
Has this been stupid

Stupid am I to care
Stupid I am to devote
Myself to the feelings of others
Opening my heart to pain

Many times in my life
I have fallen for a lady
Almost every time
I have been a fool

Not necessarily purposefully
Understand, I am self-aware
But never have I met anyone
That returns the feelings and care

Many times in my life
I have been a fool
I have been a fool most recently
After swearing off the pursuit

Happiness is not defined by another
And yet, I feel a fool
I feel a fool for feeling
My happiness wrongly defined

Many times in my life

I have sworn off being a fool
Never again I will proclaim
Only to be a fool again

It may take a month
It may take five years
But eventually
The fool is unchained

I have always felt this way
Always the same old taste
Just renewed injuries
Scars reopened and bleeding

Many times in my life
I have felt the fool
If it is to be my end
Then I will die the fool

For pursuit of love is not foolish
Though it may feel
To be loved is to be acknowledged
As a worthy human being

For what else is there in life
What else is there to drive
Motivations pure, to feel alive
To live one's life

As a fool
It's all quite cruel

DARK DEPTHS

Here we are all of us
Floating, but froth atop
The dark depths of life
Carried by currents and swell
At the mercy of life's tide

Here we float, we lucky few
Simultaneously experiencing
Dark waters gloom
Up and down, we undulate
As we float, prostrate

Staring into endless gloom
How do we get on with it
Without pondering our doom
It seems, small mindedly
We have created bubbles of our own

In our bubbles we are content
Floating universes of our own
Each perceived by others, unknown
But interconnected and entwined
We occupants oblivious

Some people see beyond the bubble
See all the others heading the same way
To an end, where all bubbles are popped
Occupants surprised to note
It has all come to an end

Thus, in our bubbles we must be free
Experience our own little universes
For all bubbles don't last eternity
That is for the dark waters
Not for us, the froth the conscious

A LIFETIME

It takes a long time
Whispers at nighttime
It takes a long time to
Realize what we see
Daily

It takes a lifetime
It may take longer
Whispers at nighttime
It takes time to see
Beauty

It takes a long time
It can take a short time
Mostly though, it's a long time
To see what we miss
Amidst the pines

It takes a lifetime
To see what we had
Whispers in the nighttime
Turn in screeches in daytime
Vibrance all around

It doesn't have to take a lifetime
It can take a short time
Whispers at nighttime
Tell us what we should see
Daily, daily

Pushing up daisies
It took a lifetime
To become the beauty
That whispers at nighttime
Flowers in the glory

It took a lifetime
Whispers in the nighttime
To live through a lifetime
Just to reach the same
Finish line

THE DEVILS BALLROOM

In the darkness, red lit
Our tormented souls dance
Swirling red dresses and crisp suits
The demons tune driving all
Rhythmic and determined

Demons dance among us
All dressed, suits and dresses too
Hidden from our view, with us all the same
Who is your partner in the ballroom
Do you even know?

In the devil's ballroom
All will be revealed in time, for those vigilant
But time is all but a construct
Dancing is all we have now
Never knowing with whom we swing

Red and black images swim by
Twirling as confetti in the wind
Each a person, or a demon
Each with their own intention
Black curtains glow with red backlight

As the pace intensifies
So does the heat
The room glowing, heat haze rising
We swim in eternal horror

Sweltering in our dances

As we melt in the heat, souls tormented
The demon's pace increases, beats crushing
The heat, sun hot, surrounds all
Demons' excitement intensifies
As our souls begin vaporizing

They laugh and cackle, their mirth unrestricted
Our souls their air, we never knew
Who was which, and which was who
We all dance with our demons
It's up to us to recognize

Which will dance us into vapor
Whom can we leave to save our souls

CATTLE BATTLE

In the fields they roam
Apparently carefree, at peace
Chewing sweet grass
Not holding back the gas

Docile they appear
From a distance they are a wonder
A heard of many individuals
All sweetly mooing and eating

Little did we know, at all
They plot their revenge total
They know they end up a steak, burger
From under us they plan mass murder

Seemingly unprovoked attacks begin
At random, no clear pattern at all
Walking past you were, minding yourself
When the cows came, you weren't prepared

They trample, chase, and push off cliffs
Those that unknowingly grew their number
They slowly kill us off, one by one
Or two by two, when all we hear is moo

You may think this is tripe
But that's what they want you to think
The cows are in charge
We are nothing to them at all

So slow was their plan

They hatched a new one, attrition
To raise the temperature globally
Their cute toots being our undoing

As they warm the world
They plan their genocide
Our bones will fertilize
The grass for future cows to graze

This plan will never come to fruition
We eat them, no doubt we have won the war
But to some there is nothing more terrifying
Than a cow at the front door

MOM

To be a mother is not an easy task
Not that I have experience in this
But I do have a mom, and so do you
Some have had a torrid life
Filled with stress and strife
We take for granted their gifts

It would serve us all to remember
Their sacrifices for our lives
Some have given up time
Others money and power
Many more have given up themselves
For us children to empower

Many have given us all we have
Even if we don't recognize
This has happened, almost constantly
For a mother is all we really have
Some fathers are there to help, most I am sure
I know in my case, this was not true

My mother has given all she has
Not once, twice, but over and over
All for her children, raised without dads
Neither was her choice, one amazing man
One less than ideal
But for her children she would go to the end of the world

I owe everything to my mother
When I was small, I knew she was sad

Struggling in her life alone with me
Giving all she had for me
As she worked and worked and had no fun
I knew she was sad deep in her heart

What can a small boy do
But say good night, love you
See you in the morning, the most important thing
I had to hear her say it back
As though a promise was being made
That tomorrow she would be there still
Not take the easy way out

Here we are, many years later
She still carries pain in her soul
I know of your sacrifices, Mom
I love you to the end
Thank you for taking the hard way
And making me who I am

AMORY

Oh, to be six years old
To be carefree and absorbed
In minor squabbles with friends
Made to appear huge
Everything is huge when you're
Six years old

Oh, to have a loving mother
A mother that means everything
A mother that will do anything
The center of your universe
As you're the center of hers
There is only one home
When you're six years old

Oh, to be six years old
The smallest gift means the most
To give a small gift in return
A stone, a flower, a small
Beloved toy, to return the love
You have received
To be six years old, and feel gratitude
Feel loved, and safe

Oh, to have a safe home
To have a loving family
To have all you need
To be loved by all
Everyone listens to what

You have to say even when
You have nothing to say
In particular

Oh, to be six years old
To be surrounded by friends
Playing on the swings
Wearing shoes or not
No one notices your feet
Soft pads on hard turf and tar
Oh, to be six, and not worry

Oh, to be six years old
Loved by all and loving all
Playing, giggling, and running
Hair blowing in the wind
If only we could remember those days
Those who loved us so
The time we had to ourselves
The love from our parents
Carefree

Six years old

DESPAIRING

Desolate landscape, cloud covered
Wind blown
Frost accumulating around rocks
No life to be seen, no green
Nothing moves but for the wind

Baking deserts, sands simmering
Swirls of dust blown in sweltering heat
Moisture but a dream of times past
No life to be seen, no green
Nothing moves but for the wind

Airless rocks devoid of colour
Pitted and pelted by tiny stones and dust
Ever finer grains cling to each other
No life to be seen, no green
Nothing moves

The vacuum in my soul worsens
Slowly consuming itself in a swirling miasma
Soon, soon nothing will remain
Ever thinner and more transparent
Nothing can live with this

Wisps of soul twirl and dance
As dust in the desert wind
Thinning, receding as the hair
On an aged head, a forest losing trees
Nothing can live here, barren

As soul evaporates, so does hope
Cold, dry, airless, and hopeless
The vacuum grows in power
Emptiness winning out over volume
Something becoming nothing in a breath

I am gone now, once a nebula of joy and hope
All that remains is void
Vacuum, nothingness, cold
No sparks will heat my soul
For there is no soul to heat

BOPANDA

Never will you know the joy
The pure life and happiness
You bring to this world

It cannot be viewed from the source
Your influence on us all immeasurable by you
But we all know it, feel it, love it

You bring love and cheer to the world
You bring tales of woe and wonder
For those lucky few who listen

Every day in your life is a gift
Every day in your presence treasured
Never have you caused pain

Never will you cause pain
Your soul too amazing
Pure good, purity of life and light

I hope you know you're special
A truly spectacular person
A beauty beyond our ken

SILVER GOLD MOON

Floating on emptiness
Between objects of insane mass
Pulling at each other across the gulf
We touch...

Suffocate the pain in this vacuum
Pulled apart by nothing
Ebbing and flowing love
Like a winters cold snap
Under a still silver gold moon

Sparks of glory resonate
In from our energetic contact
Threatening to shatter our emotions
All the while floating in nothing

No breath to be had in this space
This place suffocates all
Who dare wander its paths
As the moon pays silent witness
To our loves destruction

Our love changes phase
Solid to liquid
Flowing between us viscous in nature
Flash boiling as our intensity increases

Drown as the liquid enters lungs
No breath to be had as it coats surfaces
Self is lost in the moment

As we twirl under
The silver gold moon's silent stare

Single out the emotion
As it filters through your pores
Covering skin with a vibrant sheen
Only we can see as we float

Colours explode all over
Skin as the sheen bends light
Flashing and dimming into eternity
Threatening to blind observers
Reflecting the beauty of the silver gold moon

OBNOXIOUS THUNDER

Happiness enters
And all else fades

As you enter the room
The world is muted

Nothing else matters
When you are around

As even the loudest noise
Passes without a sound

With the world blocked out
By your glorious wonder

I have to ask
How will I blunder

All else falls asunder
And you leave the room

The world returns
With obnoxious thunder

I'M THROUGH

Why should I care?
Soft flesh...
Broken by teeth
Oozing life blood

Sharp teeth
Encasing the softest heart
Its broken now...

I don't get it now...
All this pain
Why is it that
It hurts
When love is there

I just don't get it
Sharp teeth
Crushing this heart
Squeezing the life out
But why now?

Don't even look at me
I'm ashamed
It hurts to care
But I do all the same
Pull away from me
Just one more time

Who is it that tunes this
Instrument of love

It's all out of whack
And sounds bad
Don't respond

It's not alright to cry
But it is alright to want to
Die in this world
Swallowed by pain

When you moved into
My heart that day
It was the start of wonder
And the pain

I'm through.

SINKING

I shall spend eternity
Trapped inside her eyes
A prison of comfort
And eternal beauty

Locked away sinking into her
Delving deeper than emotion may follow
Blood coursing through my veins
A haze veiling the beautiful world

Her eyes are a shade of sea green
Beautifully seductive and expressive
My only regret
Is my inability to be with her

Soaking through me as dazzling light
Blinds me in my end
I fear I may not survive
This world without her

Eyes stare through everyone
Seeing through lies and mindless folly
Her gaze makes me fly
Far from this retched reality

If only we could be together
If only life was made of heaven
An unreachable reality
Torn apart like a shattered dream

I hear crying

As my tears fall to the floor
Dropping water in dust where life is void
I can't continue down this path

There can be an end to suffering
My hell can be defeated
Tailored nightmares erased
But not in this lifetime

Not by myself

DROWNING

I wonder what would have been
Had he continued along his path
He was wondering along a lost trail
Ending in death

He lost his way
He was on the fast track
But he floated off
On a river of substance

It caused him pain
He tried to push through
It was fun for a time
Lost in fake bliss

The facade of liquid
Blinding him...
Impairing his judgment
He went together
Tangled in a web

He kept it around as comfort
In the end it killed him
Rivers of his blood flowing
Through the streets
He felt himself sliding
Empty through those streets

He opened another
Drank it quick

And thought of quitting
Drank it quick
And thought of her

TO MY KNEES

Meet me here in my bones
It is warm and without pressure
Gliding together in this goodness
Created from nothing
Something comes for real

Here in my lungs
Blackened with hatred and pain
You clear up the fog of misconception
As we glide here in the flame
Everlasting warmth surrounds

Lover, to my knees is the cry
Cooling off in the shade of the bottle
Emptied by lust but filled with love
For the air we share in this
Our kingdom of peace

Sit with me in this heaven
Shine down upon them as we smile
Your sweet embrace is here to
Keep us together in life
And death

The first of our lives
Shared in this calm of autumn leaves
Sit down and shine with me
Beautiful goddess of mine
Fill my heart with love

Lungs breathing your smell
Infusing feeling abounds
All around us in our piece of existence
Obtaining a peace dreamed of by all
On this earth

Storms skirt us
Impenetrable in our being here
Calm waters surround our wake
As we float upon our love
In this ocean of dreams

Wake up in uncomfortable light
The light with which you glow
Blinding to all
Unaccustomed to your beauty
Don't blind me with your eyes

I try
I really do try for you
I will not fail you
Glorious beauty
Sea green eyes shattering my heart

In this dreamscape...
We live forever.

CREATION OF SADNESS

A new kind of sadness
Fills her being
She wishes she was free
To be herself once more

Somethings wrong with you
You tear her apart like
She has no being
She wants to keep you
But you throw it all in her face

A new kind of upset
Fills her heart
As it is shredded
By your insecurity

Somethings wrong with you
As you throw her aside
She deserves better
But you like her pain

A new kind of sickness
Fills her stomach
She has love for you
Yet you display only hatred

There're some things wrong with you
You feed on depression

You eat all her sadness
And replace it with hatred

A new kind of pain
Resides in her heart
As you broke it to pieces
And fed off her empty plate

Somethings wrong with you
You don't feel her pain
You make her so sad
Yet you are happy and free

A new kind of hatred
Fills her existence
You created her hell
Now she has to die

Somethings wrong with you
You kill all her goodness
And make her a husk
You make her all numb

A new kind of nothing
Spreads through her soul
She is dead
And she has you to thank

Somethings wrong with you
You killed off her everything
And fed on the nothing
That makes you irresistible

FADE AWAY

Put back your heart
It's needed for the journey
If it's left behind
Who will save your life?

I'll try
But I'm locked out
I can't enter your cell
I think I can try...
I will save your life

If I fail, I will die
I will lose myself and cry
Why did I even try
Your heart is lost
And I'll fade away

Put back your heart
It's needed for our journey
I love you, and I saved your life
As you saved my life in the end

End it now
I feel you close
I'm anxious to be closer to you
But you are untouchable
I feel I am losing you

After all
I never had you in the end

You've drained my life
Empty

HEAVY RAIN

She sleeps
And we dance
In this world
We take it all away

She sleeps
And we wait for her
As she sleeps
We clown around
Waiting for her...

She sleeps
We can't wait anymore
She sleeps
In this rain
Patience past and present
No more

She wakes
We wait to hear her answer
We wait
In this deluge of emotion
Soaked to the core
Wet no more

She answers
And the clouds erupt
Joy flowing freely
Anxiously we wait
The feeling never passes

She answers
The rain won't go away
She won’t stop it for us
Hair soaked and clinging
Clothes drenched
Nothing matters

She comes inside
Tells us the truth
The rain stops
And sun shines through
Her buoyant hair

We wait no more
As the truth is exposed
It rains no more
As feelings come to the fore
We wait no more

NIGHT CATS

As the sun sets
On a hot summers day
The cats emerge from hibernation
To frolic and play

To and fro, fast and slow
Creeping in the still warm dark
Prey beware, hunters are about
Do fear, they may be cute

But deadly are they
Rats, snakes and all between
Run away, for you may scream
A cat upon you is death, certain

In the darkness they lurk
Eyes the colour of pitch
All the better to see you with
Far from the animal whose parents do scritch

Up trees and in bushes they prowl
Not even afraid of the dark, a pure night owl
Out at the club of the Red Cat Flap
Partying away and causing general crap

Ah, but dusk doth cometh, home must the feline go
To pretend to starve and wake their owner
Who is the pet and who is the slave?
Only a cat will truly know

They bend us to their will, you see

For daytime cuteness transfixes us meekly
But at night the true cat will appear
To blood upon your walls smear

A fresh coat of paint, they think
Mayhem written in the font of victim
Only for their loving owner to appear
Screaming oh no, oh dear

But Fluffles is now asleep on her chair
About the paintwork and night before not to care
She has her way and always will
A feline certainly is a jagged pill

WITH REGRET

When I am old
When life has grown cold
I will look back
As would an author
Reviewing his story
And I will know
I should have spent more time
Smiling and laughing with you
My last regret
Will draw out my last tear

SAVE ME (FROM MYSELF)

Snakes envelope me
Serpents of dire feel
Slippery and insidious
Biting my flesh and
Consuming my soul

I feel abandoned
By myself and others
A waste of life
A wasted life
A fool taking up space

It feels like no one
Wants me around
Like I should be confined
By the serpents of my own making
My soul consumed by them all

I feel I've twisted and contorted
I've become something I hate
Though I always loved being alone
Now it is my prison
Barred by hatred and self-loathing

It feels like no one will help
I cannot help myself this time
Those I love do not love me back
I am an irritation, a scab to be picked off

A tick on the side of a unicorn

Surviving on scraps of blood
Of a magnificent beast
But you aren't what you eat, after all
I'm a parasite on an angel
I pair of concrete shoes

One size to fit all for those
Would be friends I weigh down
An irritation to be tolerated
An itch to be salved
A rash to be cured

Someone help me
I cannot help myself this time
This is not a happy place
For a soul to live
It should be put out of its misery

WASHED AWAY

First the waves come
Pounding relentless
An unsubtle caress of power
Washing away all

You should know by now
I couldn't make it work
I don't have the strength
To resist them

The waves come
And wash us all
Away
Into our deathbeds

Then will come the wind
Scattering out dusted bone
To all parts asunder
A storm of bones blasting all

The waves continue on and on
An endless crashing and receding
Crashing and receding
Crashing and receding

No one left to witness the shore
No shells remain in their wake
In this new realm, only black stone
Covers beaches once golden

The waves come

And the tides go
But the waves never stop
Dreary skies over dead earth

Dark waters cover all
In the end only our bones
Are blown in the wind
The waves crash and recede

Crash and recede
Crash and recede
Crash and recede
For eternity

HOLLOW

I walk through this life
Somniferous eyes cast over all
I am tired, can't breathe, tired of it all
They all look through me, like not here
Not here at all, some spectral ghost

I float around, always circling lives
Never to become part, never involved
Unwanted, burdened with solitude
Those I've loved have walked right through me
Left a hole in my soul, almond shaped and gaping

A wound that won't heal, close over time
Festering dark deep inside me, a hole
Into the oblivion of the universe
Those that I have loved, reached for, adored
Ignore and cast a long shadow over life

I'd write down all the pain
I'd call someone, but have no one to call
And I forgot my pen somewhere
I hate to be the burden on the others
Those that have left me behind

Those that I circle, those I orbit
I have no gyroscope to keep me level
The hole has taken the whole
Made it incomplete, incomprehensible
Now those I love simply pass through

A spectral anomaly, something unseen, intangible
Like the love I feel for some, felt for others
Now a specter of my past, a shadow of
What could be, what could have been
What will never be, for me

Even as my shelter is safe
I lie alone in the darkness
Weight of life crushing my bones
As I live vicariously through others
Watching and trying to be real
Be a person that could be loved

But I cannot, for there is something wrong
Deep inside me, a black hole of a scar
Sucking in all, passing right through me
And out the other side, love like
Water off a duck's back, always to run off

So, I walk through this life
Tired, breathless, and aged beyond my time
My spark is waning, humor defying me, leaving me cold
All I can do is look on, loving from a distance, always
Never to be involved

Undeserving of love, care, connection
Like an old broken telephone
Peaceful in background storage, mourning times past
Alone in the dark, I lie and want to cry
But I cannot, for I don't know what I cry for

It has been taken by the hollowness inside
Feeling love from the outside abstracted, air gapped
No hope for me, leave me here, I will die alone
This I know for sure, I will die alone
No one will be there to care, or remember

The shadow that passed through their lives

The specter they passed through and felt cold
That odd feeling as though it has hailed
Sudden cold that passes by
As I pass on into the darkness
And become one with my only friend

No Eden for me, no respite
All that awaits in the end is the endless
The darkness of eternity
I feel it already
In that hollow hole in my soul

LIFE BEFORE

Life before was easier
In a way
Life before was simpler
Then I met you

You changed it all
Showed me what was possible
What I should be
How I could be

But knowing this I look back
Knowing that you'll never be mine
You still make my life shine
Even if all I can do is watch you

I'll always want more
Though I'll never get it
I'll taste your name
And you'll taste mine

But to think there would be more
Would make me out of my mind
I love you to death
But death is all I will have in the end

Your light shines down
Brightening my day every day
Its barbaric, in a way
That I should suffer such delight

We've always been so close

And yet so far
So loving and caring
And yet so distant

That is how life is now
Life before was simpler
But worse
For your absence

HERE WE GO

We all see the news
Hearing and witnessing everything at once
Doomed to waste in this dystopia
We never saw it coming, but here it is
It's what we have now

We are everywhere
We experience all these catastrophic events
Together and simultaneously
Many always happened, but locally
Globalization has made us more aware

We consider it all a threat, even local events
Across the world and continents away
We all think it's the end, it is nigh
But it's always been this way and always will
How can you say this is the end?

When it is, you may know, and you may not
You may be here one minute
Gone the next, unfeeling if you're fortunate
No one will show you the end, it will just come
It's all an illusion until it isn't anymore

As are you, an illusion, a dream of the universe
Dreaming of itself, a bubble of awake
Dreaming of being woke
While in the end, nothing will matter
You will be gone, and so will I and everyone else

Dust in the wind, dust among the stars
Stop watching the news
Don't buy into the hate
All we have is now and each other
This moment, this breath

Change is coming, it is inevitable
As is death and decay in the end
Believe in the now, not the improbable or impossible
Not in the leader spouting lies
Not in others, but yourself

Here we go, this is the start
Not the end.

SHOWER

Set the water just right
Temperature just below scalding
Pressure, relentless
Prepare to wash away the day

Live in the moment
Hot water washing away
The sins and triumphs of
The day passed

Burning away grime and time
Scented soap to bring you back
Olfactory memories of showers past
Stay in this moment

The moment is all you have
Wash your hair, long or short
Take the time to massage
Your tired skull, filled with thoughts

Morning or night
Personal choice, there is not wrong
Cleanse the body, free your soul
Sins down the drain regardless

Let the water pummel you
Burn you into the present
The present is all we have
And we never know

Remembering past horrors

Reliving past pleasures
Planning tomorrow
Next week, next month

Now is all there is
In the hot shower
The one time we have peace
Time to ourselves

Sleep doesn't count, dreams betray
The sanctity of our subconscious
Shower time is conscious
Routine, uninterrupted

Now is all we have
Keep that in mind next time
You're showering, ritualistic in repetition
Now is all there is

SACRED SILENCE

When the world is quiet
When the work is done
Or time has blessed me with time
I think of you, of course
Only you, and always you

You have invaded my thoughts
Grown into my heart as roots
Of the giant redwood grow deep
Into the nourishing earth
You have grown into my very soul

Without you in my mind
There would be nothing
Emptiness, void, imploding skull
Nothing to keep the dark at bay
Heart would stop, no roots, supporting structure

I wish I could show you how I see you
Show you your true self, how you shine
How you banish the dark
As did the first star in the universe
As does the sun each day, rising high

I wish you could feel as I do
For not only you but for me
I wish I knew your thoughts as I know mine
See myself through your eyes
Know the delight or disgust

But I am the earth, and you the tree
You grow beautiful and luscious
Blooming and growing, while I feed you
My very soul your nourishment
Your lifeblood, my heart provides

You will never know how the earth cared
As I will the earth never know how the tree felt
Growing from the foundation of love unknown
The earth will do anything for the tree
And the tree with live forever happy

Oblivious of the earth
The earth forever silent
The tree forever sacred

STARING AT THE QUEEN

Stood
As though carved from granite
Stood
Unable to move
Transfixed

Stood
Static and unbreathing
Stood
As breathtaking beaty looks back
Stood

Speechless, unable to find the words
Stood
Staring at her
She is all there is
And I am but marble

Stood
In the pouring rain
Stood
Drenched, in glory and rain

Stood there
I can't move
Can't speak
Can't think
Transfixed by her, awestruck

Stood
Like a fool
Stood there
As one stares without comprehension
Stood, not knowing upon what I gaze

She has it all
The world in her palm
My heart in the other
Stood still, I can't move
Afraid if I will

She will go, as the breath I exhale
Blown away in the wind
Never to be seen again
Stood, I won't move
I will stare at her forever

DESCENT

It feels as though I have descended
From the point of origin, happy
To a point of darkness, alone
My thoughts darkening
As this work has grown and grown

I've looked back, you see
Taken works from past efforts
Refitted them and shone them up
Created new works, happy
And slowly descended

Madness and depression eating
Into creativity that was happy
Now I am a sad fool
Repeating the same old cliché
Working hard at working
Creating sadness instead

I was hoping this work would be good
A balance of happiness and sad
Balance of good and evil
Dancing with our demons as we do
But it seems the demons are leading
The band reached crescendo

And here I dance alone
Spilling out poison as I go
Dreaming of what I don't have
Dreaming of happiness

While you read this and soak up
Sanguine sadness

For this I apologize, you see
It was not my intention
I can be funny, I can be happy
But in the end, the clichéd tortured artist
Comes to the fore

Here I sit, preparing my anthology
Sparing time to give an apology
The age-old battle, remain consequential
Long in tooth, perhaps, relevance questionable
We all battle this, I know
But the descent continues

BEATINGS

Teenage years gave me a beating
One I never recovered from
Here I still struggle, twenty years on
Still fighting the old battles
Scarred within my soul

Pride was robbed
Soul cracked up
Mind was hurt, never to recover
But here I am, and where are they?

Bullying is a terrible truth
It should be handled better
You would think we would know how
You would think we could protect our children
And teach them not to be horrible
Teach them not to be hurt

But we cannot, even now
The more sensitive the child, the greater the damage
I'm not saying most are standing idly by
But we should be better
Especially those of us that went through hell

I got here, I don't know how
Others are not so lucky
I knew a girl at school, she was lovely
A year below me, but I knew her
She killed herself because of bullies in my year

She couldn't handle that she loved her bully
And her bully didn't know how to feel loved
Look how it ended, hanging by her school tie
Horrific, I would have liked to have known her better
But now no one will

Bullying robs us all; it is a battle we must win
A war we must overcome
It is not a rite of passage
It is not character-building
It is soul destroying
Life changing

The world is robbed by bullies
Don't stand for it, I know I won't
Bully someone I care for now
Bully me now, I dare you
You won't win again

You won't win again with me.

ANOTHER YEAR

As another year draws to a close
We all rejoice in our break from work
In the end we live at work and visit
Fleetingly, our homes

As the year comes to a close
This changes, we live at home
We have more fun, relax
Spend time with those we love
If we are lucky, and spend time with those
That perhaps love us

As the year comes to a close
Tensions run higher and higher
Rushing to finish our tasks and work
Before the close of business
Rushing and working our lives away
For a brief break before we do it again

As the year comes to a close
We look back on it in dismay
For it was January yesterday
And will be tomorrow
And then December will follow
Close behind, always looming
Then another January

Too quickly do our years come to a close
All too brief are our lives
Work punctuated by life

Drudgery and sweat punctuated by passion
We waste this time we have

We really do.

TORMENT OF DREAMS

My dreams torment me
They tease of what I could have
Who I could be with

I have spent more time
With people I care about in dreams
Than in the waking world
That is torment, that is betrayal

Dreaming of those we love
From a distance, never to touch
But to spend time with them in dreams
Laughing and loving, caring and smiling
Makes the waking world hurt

Dreams are where I would rather be
Forever dreaming of those I love
For in my dreams they love me back
They care for me as I do for them
I am happy in my dreams

Then I wake up
All I want to do is stay in the dream
Memories of happiness and togetherness
Flitting through my mind
Remembered, fortunately and sadly
I wish I could sleep forever

Dream of you forever
Dream of her forever

Spend time with you all
Love and be loved
Dream be damned, it is better there

Better to dream oblivious
Of the struggles of the waking world
Better to be dreaming of her
It is only when I awake
That the betrayal is complete

I will go through that day
Wishing for my dreams
Wishing for them to be true
Only to be disappointed daily
End up wishing for sleep

To return to the realm in which I am happy
The realm where she holds my hand
The realm she tells me she cares too
The realm in which I smile
Laugh and sing in the sun

Holding her dreamt-up hand
Is better than living this life
Awake and alone

SOLITUDE

Oh solitude, my garden prison
Constructed for defense and safety
Trapping me in this hell
Solitude, my sweet hateful mistress
I gave you everything and you took it all
Took everything from me

Solitude, my beautiful jail
I made you myself I know
We dance our dance, I hold your bars
Swing from them like a trapped animal
A mistress of my own creation
My precious private hell

You're all mine, and I am yours
We are tied together forever
One made the other
Tricked into thinking it was smart
A barrier from pain
Only to realize all too late
There is no going home now

Well built, this prison
Customized for my benefit
Cracks may appear, but like defenses of old
They are built to last, these walls
Cracks are but a surface feature
A decoration for the cell
Nothing to write home about

If writing home was possible

I will wait here forever
Safely trapped in my own prison
My customized, personally created hell
Sadly confined, ready to escape
Too afraid to leave
I will watch the world from within
Smiling at the others, at the view
Shedding a tear for placing myself here

In my personal cage.

NEAR OCEANS

When the seas closed upon them, the whales sang. Deep within, they swam. Deep within, they dream.

Miasma swam with her mother, Diaspora, deep within the swells of the Ruddy Depths. Her flukes feeling the pressure of a thousand atmospheres, unknowingly of course, she swam. Panting in the gases needed for life. Diaspora, many times her age, swept down upon the feeding wake. Their mouths agape, they consumed. Only one hundred and three rotations old, Miasma was but a young one amongst the elders, dutifully readying herself for the coming of age. She was ready to meet a male of mating age but was yet to know one. All she had known through her ages of immaturity was consumption and growth.

Her growth, now near-full, was quite on schedule. Her mother had been preparing her for her meeting with a potential mate, though she had never met a male of her kind. She was quite excited, as to be biologically expected, and was ever-keen to meet a new fellow whale. Miasma had not even known her father, as her mother Diaspora had not known hers, as was the way of the whale. As ever deeper through the Ruddy Depths they swam, her excitement at the approaching experience grew. She had not known the meeting nor the mating, though as she was informed neither had her mother and indeed nor her grandmother. Apparently the ways of the whale were blind.

On her one hundred and seventh rotation, as deep in the Ruddy Depths as she had ever travelled, she met her mate. She only knew this by the subtle difference in the feeling of the Depths - a spicy scent, perhaps one invoking a feeling of calm vermillion. Her mother enticed her to swim deeper, ever deeper, as she progressed. Thicker and thicker became the Ruddy Depths. Eventually, after passing the depth where feeding was no longer possible, she located her mate. They met, swimming in instinctual concert, swirling in a helix through the dense medium surrounding them. They briefly touched, ever so fleeting, long enough however for material to pass, the material and instruction for new life crossing between. Suddenly, Miasma felt the urge to flee, repulsed by her mate and their intimate dance, as he appeared to react similarly. She started to swim up, back up to the living feeding grounds above where her mother awaited.

As was their way, following finding her mother in the Ruddy Depths and continuing her perpetual feeding, her body began to incubate the combined material that had passed in the mating. This she instinctively knew would take much time, and she knew her mate was undergoing the same growth. As was the way with their kind, the males bore males, while the females bore females. Her daughter would one day grow to her age now and have her first mating, and on life would go. Almost a full rotation following the mating, it was time. Swimming to the upper limit of the feeding range of the Ruddy Depths, where it was sometimes possible depending on time and condition to see at least a few of the various moons in the sky, she went through the painfully joyous moments of birth, and her first daughter was born. As it was a particularly clear and dark time, she would name her Marble after the great moon floating in the sky.

Miasma and Marble swam slowly down to once again meet up with Miasma's mother, taking time for Marble to acclimatise to the pressure as they went. It would take some time for her to become accustomed and strong enough to swim at greater and greater depths where pressure was immense. After some time, she met with her mother and some other females feeding at what would be the higher end of their usual channel, having swum up to meet up with Miasma and her daughter on the way down, excited to meet the new female joining them. Marble approached her grandmother with love and excitement, instinctively recognising Miasma's mother among the others. Miasma took up formation alongside Marble, now flanked by grandmother and mother for protection and guidance.

Many rotations passed, Miasma having failed to meet another mate as yet and her only daughter Marble now approaching the age Miasma was when she had begun her first journey into the mating depths, and Diaspora was becoming sluggish. She could no longer consume as consistently as when she was younger as her body aged and began to break down. She was always now among the last to follow the rest of the whales up or down through the Ruddy Depths. Eventually, after more than a rotation of slowing and beginning to struggle, she passed. Her great eyes closed for the last time, no longer able to see her kind and glimpse the moons in the sky, and she slowly began to sink away from the rest of the group. Miasma was distressed by the loss of her mother, her guiding beacon through the ages of her life. Her ever-present care and matriarchal companionship drew to a close.

Swimming down slowly around the remains of her mother as they sunk, circling in a fashion reminiscent to that of the mating spiral, Miasma knew she would have to guide her daughter alone now, her time as the eldest of the group was approaching and she too would have to lead them through the Ruddy Depths as they fed. She concluded this ritual farewell and returned to Marble and the others knowing all the while that the same would one day happen with her and Marble.

Ever onward would the family swim, through the Ruddy Depths and through life, undisturbed by others and undiscovered. Even as in millions of rotations the sun would swell and begin its death expansion, Jupiter would last longer than the inner planets, allowing the whales in its gaseous oceans to continue their cycles for millennia to come. Marble and her children and their children would remember forever in their profound genetic memories, instinctive and deep, the names of those before them. Diaspora, Miasma, Marble, and the others prior and to follow, would live on in dream and memory.

www.ingramcontent.com/pod-product-compliance
Lightning Source LLC
LaVergne TN
LVHW050333160826
845677LV00014B/3605

* 9 7 9 8 3 6 8 3 0 0 4 7 4 *